Love and
Empowerment

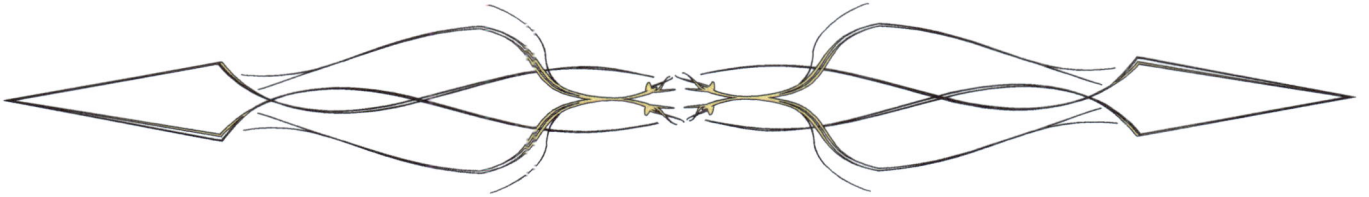

Love and Empowerment

A Compilation of Wisdom for Your Heart and Soul

Rebekah Harkness

BIONIC Press

www.bionicpressbooks.com

Cover design and illustrations by Rebekah Harkness

Copyright © 2015 by Rebekah Harkness

Published by BIONIC Press
Salt Lake City, UT 84088

Manufactured in the United States of America

ISBN: 978-0-9892448-4-8

To all those that
understand that love
and power grow from within.

We can either

AS IT

blame the

OR

don't work out

AN active ROLE

our own

accept life
comes and
WORLD
when things
we can play
in creating
REALITY.

Inner peace

is when
you are being
criticized and
don't feel the
need to defend
yourself.

DON'T LET YOUR HABITS CONVINCE YOU THAT THEY HAVE MORE POWER THAN YOU DO.

Each day
is a
GIFT.

It is our responsibility
to return the favor and
add beauty and value to
the world.

BE
OPEN
to seeing
things
differently.

It's **N** **E** **V** **E** **R** too late to say I'm sorry.

It's **NEVER** too late to admit you made a mistake.

Each day poses a new opportunity to be a better person than you were yesterday.

Faith is not hope. It is an inner knowing that if you do your part, the rest will take care of itself.

FEED YOUR MIND

WITH WHAT YOU WANT TO EXPERIENCE IN YOUR LIFE.

Trade in your wish bone for a backbone.

GRATITUDE

IS A FEELING
THAT IMMEDIATELY
TELLS THE UNIVERSE,

"MORE PLEASE."

Your biggest asset is you.

To overcome

Fear,

recognize it

then

make a

conscious

decision

to ignore
it.

You are
so much
more
than
the sum
of your
yesterdays.

Let your appreciation for life run ocean deep.

Inherit the love and blessings patiently waiting for you by choosing kindness and grace.

LOOSEN

YOUR GRIP
ON YOUR HEART.
IT CAN
WITHSTAND
MANY
BEATINGS,
BUT IT
CAN'T
WITHSTAND
BEING
SUFFOCATED.

Proactively choose compassion.

PREOCCUPY YOURSELF WITH FAITH, OPTIMISM, AND CONFIDENCE.

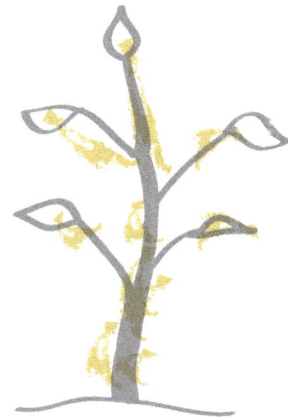

Nothing is
more *powerful*
than you.

Reclaim your power.

Talk less, love more.

YOUR HAPPI IS INDEP OF EVERYONE AROUND

NESS
ENDENT
AND EVERYTHING YOU.

YOUR
HARDEST
DAYS ARE YOUR
BIGGEST
BLESSINGS.

A new beginning guarantees you a new end.

Each and
every one of us
has a
unique gift
to give
each other
and the
world.

Sometimes
the hardest part
of creating change
is making the
decision that a
change is needed.

Acknowledge and celebrate
your small wins.
They lead you directly
to that elusive
pot of gold.

Exercise confident humility
knowing all of the good that
exists is yours for
the taking.

DON'T LEAK YOUR

ENERGY TO
MOMENTS
THAT
DON'T
EXIST.

Your attitude has more influence than your talent, money, and education combined.

Perfection isn't real.

Instead of striving for perfection,

strive to
continuously
move in the
direction of
who you
want to
become.

YOU ARE ENOUGH.

You can
only go
as far
as you
can
see.

DON'T CONTAMINATE YOUR SPIRIT

WITH THE FEAR AND PESSIMISM OF OTHERS.

Be faithful to positivity and love.

Imagine what it would be like to become who you long to be.

Believe in the strength and resiliency of your soul.

Evolve into LOVE.

See with your heart,
listen with your mind,
and feel with your soul.

PUSH YOUR STRENGTHS.

Regardless of your geographical location, your mind is your dwelling place.

Let

LOVE

rule your life.

Forgiveness opens your heart and soul to receive the countless blessings that were patiently waiting for you.

Don't get lost SEARCHING *for a happily ever*

after.

*Focus
on a
happily
after
now.*

Allow yourself to **blossom** into who you were meant to be.

E V E R Y T H I N G

reacts to you at the level you respond to it.

LIFE IS **BITTERSWEET.** *GENERATE MORE* **SWEET** *BY IGNORING THE BITTER.*

Surround

with people
that have traits
you want to
cultivate
within yourself.

yourself

There is
no one
you need
to change
besides
you.

Happiness
comes
when
your

and

agree.

HEAL YOUR MIND AND BODY WITH

forgiveness.

Inner peace

is when you observe differences in others and don't feel the need to change them.

Go
through.

ACCEPT

this moment
exactly as it is.

Recognize your inner strength and face the daily

tribulations of life with an attitude of confidence, peace, and hopeful expectancy.

Be mindful

of who you spend your time with. We tend to take on the thoughts, feelings, and habits of others that are in our inner circle.

Kindness

and

compassion

transcend

all differences.

**We create habits,
then our habits
create us.**

STOP TRYING TO BE SOMEONE ELSE.

Make the **OBJECT** of your attention.

Also the **OBJECT** of your affection.

Money doesn't grow
on trees, but
trees remind us of
many principles that
make us rich.

Never lose
sight of how much

POWER

you have
over your
circumstances.

LOVE
always
WINS.

your desires and dreams that have been hibernating in your heart.

Success
    isn't measured
    by the mind
    or based on
anyone's opinion.

Success
    is measured
    by the heart.
If you feel it,
you've made it.

Run
from the
PESSIMISTS.

There are no secrets. All energy is heard.

You
are a
LIMITLESS
SPIRITUAL
being
here to
overcome
the
limitations
of
human
life.

Spend
time
in
places
that
fill
your
soul
with

love.

Take conscious control
of your ability to create
and pay attention to
your thoughts, feelings,
and actions.

What you see
in others gives you
insight into
how you
view yourself.

SHINE

some light
and love
into the
dark hidden
corridors
of your
heart.

Life has
a way of

reminding

you what holds the most value.

underneath it all we are all the same

Make
room
for
something
better.
Let go
of the
past.

DON'T WANT, BUT RATHER, BE.

ACCEPT > YOURSELF.

Pretending
to be
happy
will never
create
happiness.

Decide what

is important

to you

then build

your whole

life

around it.

Negative thinking
seals your fate
and gives you

ZERO

chance
of creating
a positive outcome.

You are NOT A prisoner TO YOUR PAST.

Surrendering to negativity is a life sentence of mediocrity, frustration, and poor outcomes.

You
the
to your
happiness
success.

are DooR own and

*What you believe is
what you experience.*

Don't chase your dreams.
Become the dream.

Inner peace

is when you
are being
disagreed
with and
don't feel the
need to argue.

Every choice we make either pulls us closer to who we want to become or holds us hostage to our current self.

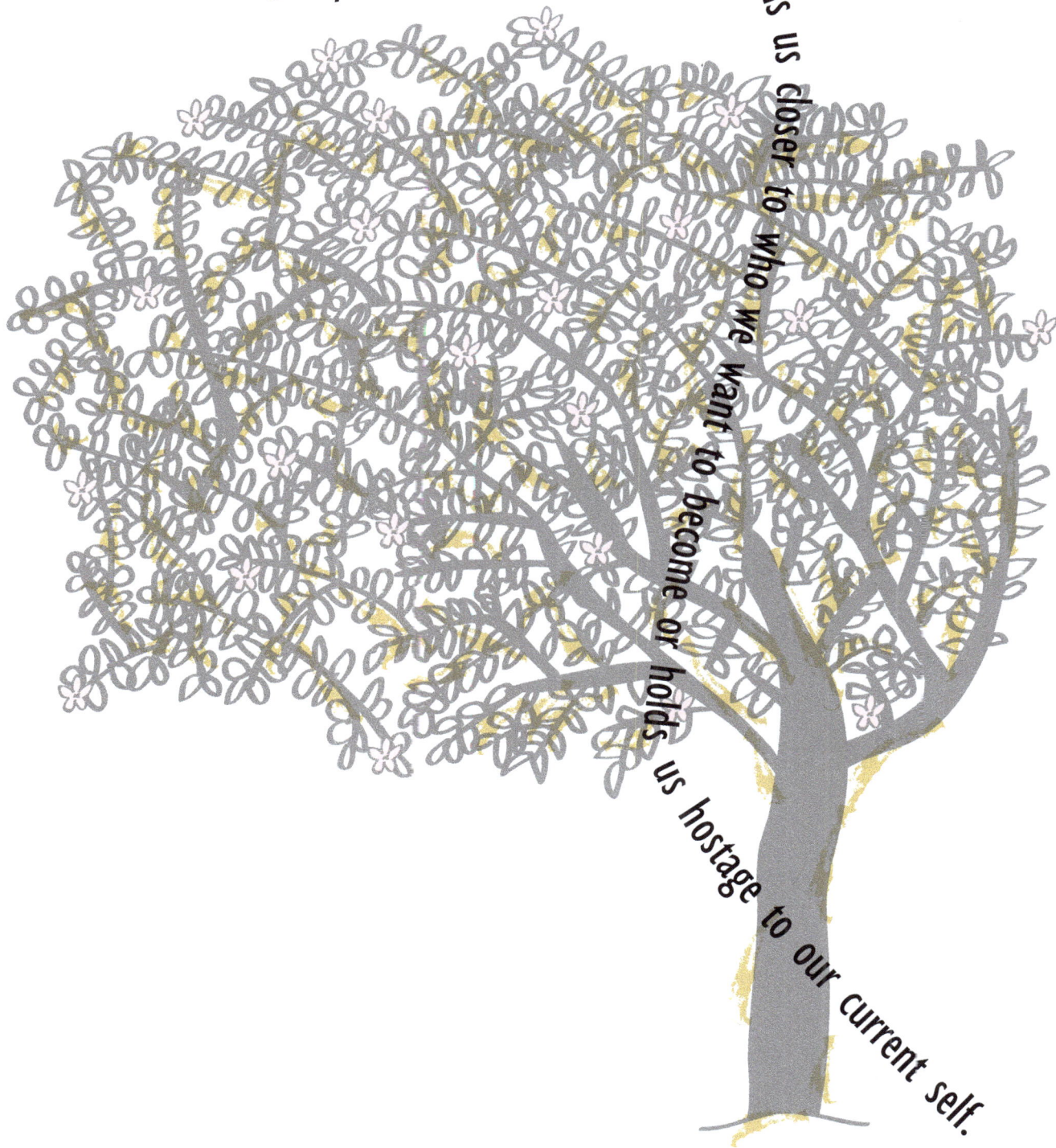

Regardless of what happened yesterday, you have an

OPPOR

TUNITY
to do
something great
today.

Fear is a thief.

Act as if you are the person you have always wanted to become.

All the beauty
in the world
gives us a small
glimpse into how
much beauty we have
within our souls.

Replace judgment with curiosity.

Do not affirm inwardly what you do NOT want to experience outwardly.

Don't put anything out into the world that you wouldn't welcome back.

If
you
are
not
sure
what
to
do,
don't act.
Keep listening.

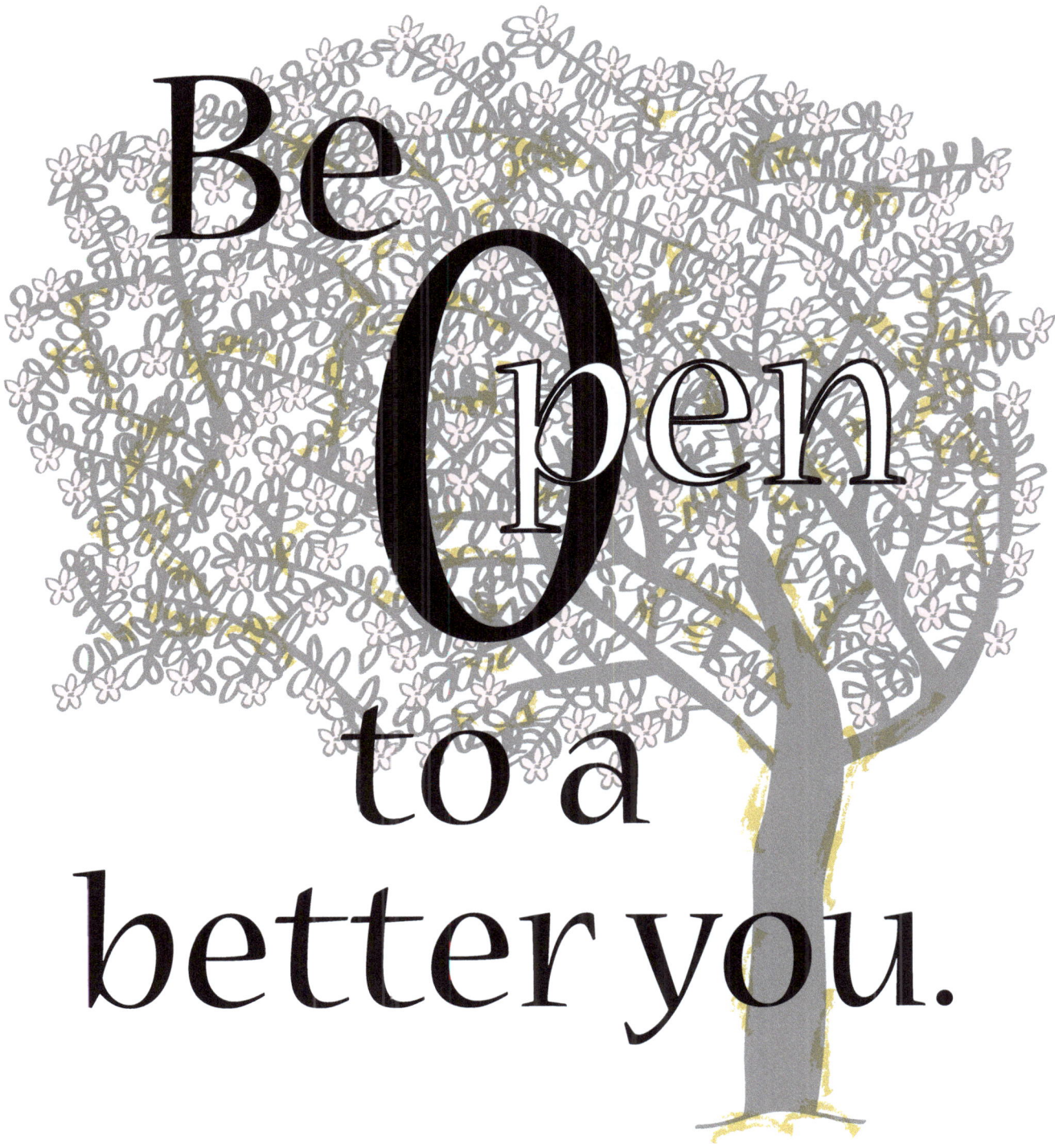

Be Open to a better you.

Live life on purpose.

SURRENDER
your mind to be
ruled by your
soul.

When you
follow
one
positive
thought

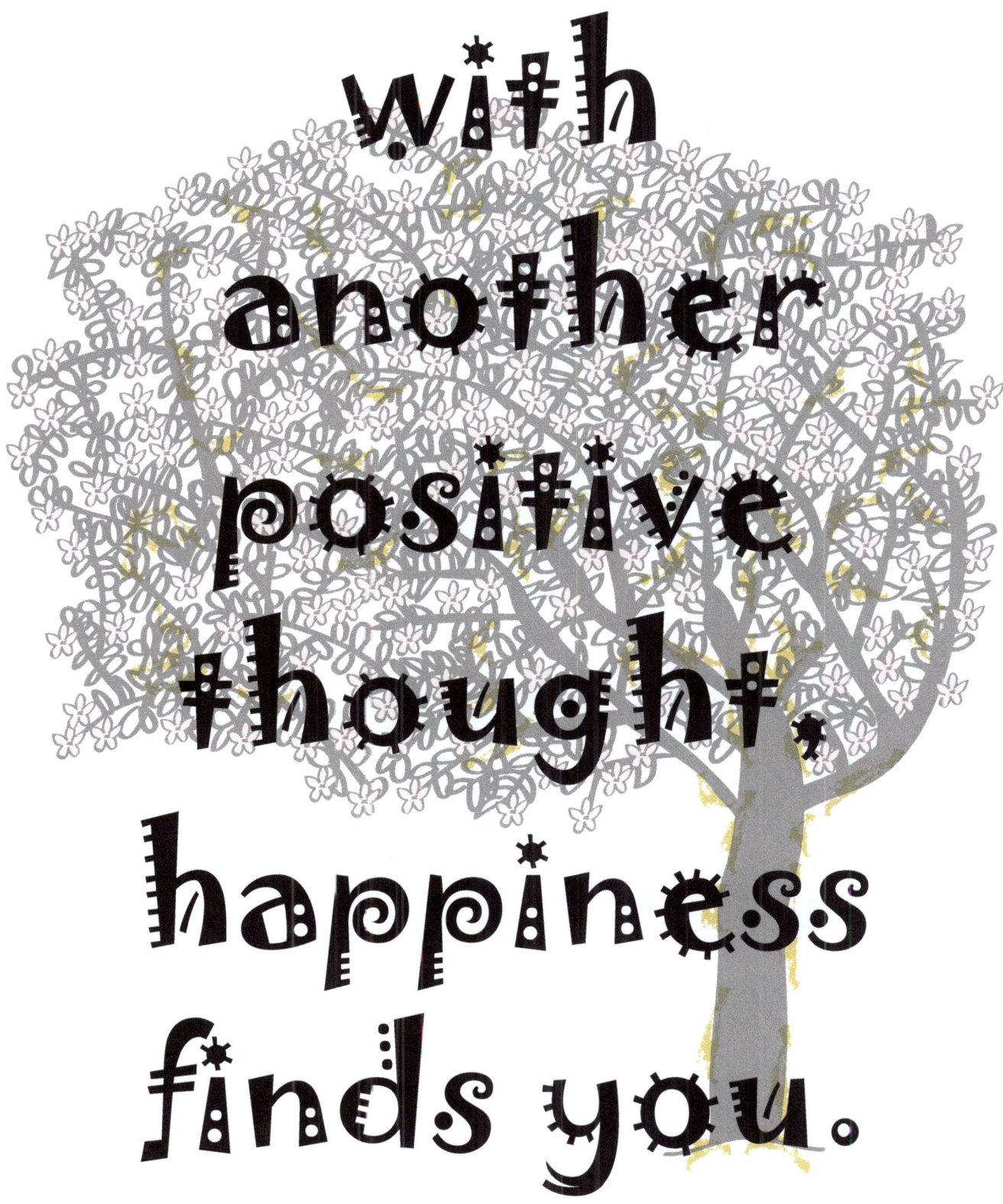

with another positive thought, happiness finds you.

You
strengthen
the whole
when you
strengthen
yourself.

Limits don't exist until you create them for yourself.

Stand up
and
have the
courage
to abandon
negativity
in your mind.

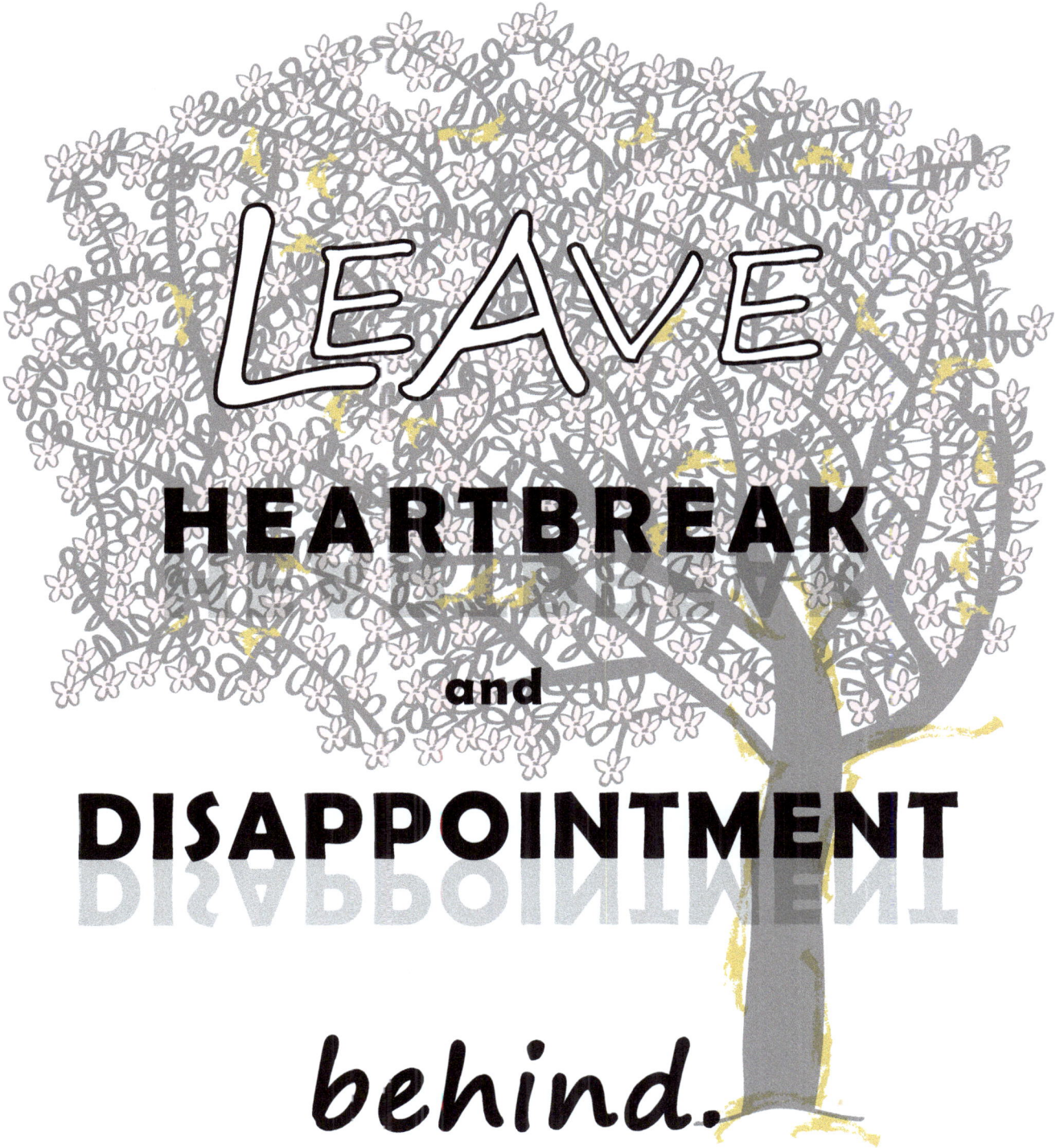

LEAVE

HEARTBREAK

and

DISAPPOINTMENT

behind.

The future is begging you to engage in *this* moment.

HAPPINESS comes when you align your decisions with what you value most in life.

Be willing to

EXPAND

your vision
of yourself.
You are

so much
stronger and
more capable
than you
think you are.

That magic
moment is
when you
feel at
peace in the
midst of chaos
and fear.

Anchor your
thoughts
in peace,
love,
compassion,
and success.

The

EGO

doesn't realize
that it is totally insane.
Bring **love** and **awareness**
to it daily.

Often times, I learn the most about

love

and companionship from my dogs.

THERE IS ALWAYS A WAY. STILL YOUR MIND AND KNOW THAT ITS ANSWERS ALWAYS WITHIN YOUR REACH.

Rejoice knowing
that the possibilities
are endless for each
and every one of us.

Fear
DIES

**when
it realizes
that it
doesn't
scare you
any more.**

Don't waste your time
FIGHTING
the opinions of others.

The past
doesn't have
to be
your
future.

Note from Author

Thank you for embracing these messages of love and empowerment. Let them percolate in your heart and mind while serving as small reminders for your soul. The illustrated growth of the cherry blossom tree brings attention to the beauty and brilliance of life. May we recognize and acknowledge the lessons of life while we celebrate it.

With much love and gratitude,

Rebekah Harkness

www.ingramcontent.com/pod-product-compliance
Lightning Source LLC
Chambersburg PA
CBHW040858100426
42813CB00015B/2842